DRONES

Space Drones

BY MARTHA LONDON

CONTENT CONSULTANT
MICHAEL BRAASCH, PHD, PE
THOMAS PROFESSOR OF ELECTRICAL ENGINEERING
OHIO UNIVERSITY

Kids Core
An Imprint of Abdo Publishing
abdobooks.com

abdobooks.com

Published by Abdo Publishing, a division of ABDO, PO Box 398166, Minneapolis, Minnesota 55439.

Printed in the United States of America, North Mankato, Minnesota
082020
012021

THIS BOOK CONTAINS RECYCLED MATERIALS

Cover Photo: JPL-Caltech/NASA
Interior Photos: US Air Force, 4–5, 6, 28; JPL-Caltech/UCAL/MPS/DLR/IDA/NASA, 8; JPL-Caltech/NASA, 10–11, 12, 15, 25, 26, 29 (bottom); Matt Deans/NASA, 16; JPL/Space Science Institute/NASA, 17; Johns Hopkins Applied Physics Laboratory, 18, 20; Swamp Works/NASA, 22–23, 29 (top)

Editor: Maddie Spalding
Series Designer: Katharine Hale

Library of Congress Control Number: 2019954181

Publisher's Cataloging-in-Publication Data

Names: London, Martha, author
Title: Space drones / by Martha London
Description: Minneapolis, Minnesota : Abdo Publishing, 2021 | Series: Drones | Includes online resources and index
Identifiers: ISBN 9781532192814 (lib. bdg.) | ISBN 9781644944417 (pbk.) | ISBN 9781098210717 (ebook)
Subjects: LCSH: Drone aircraft--Juvenile literature. | Space robotics--Juvenile literature. | Astronautics--Robot applications--Juvenile literature. | Space vehicles--Radio control--Juvenile literature.
Classification: DDC 629.435--dc23

CONTENTS

The US Air Force initially launched the X-37B drone on April 22, 2010. It has been on many missions since then.

CHAPTER 1

Exploring Space

It is August 2019. A figure glides down from the dark sky. Its wheels hit the runway. The X-37B spacecraft has returned from an **orbit** around Earth. It spent two years in space. The X-37B is a drone. A drone is an unpiloted aircraft or ship.

The X-37B drone landed at the Kennedy Space Center in Florida.

The X-37B drone is shaped like a bullet. It is 29 feet (9 m) long. Short wings stick out on its sides. It has no windows. The X-37B is the first drone to return from space and land on its own. It travels at about 17,500 miles per hour (28,200 km/h).

The US Air Force owns the X-37B. The drone's first flight was in 2010. Since then, it has orbited Earth many times. The drone has spent more than 1,000 days in orbit. The Air Force says the drone could be used to bring experiments back from space.

Flying in Space

All planets have **atmospheres**. An atmosphere is the layer of gases that surrounds a planet. Some drones have spinning blades to help them fly. The blades push against air as they spin. When a planet's atmosphere is thin, the blades have to spin faster to lift the drone. Space drones must be lightweight. If they are too heavy, they will not be able to fly.

Vesta is one of the largest asteroids. It is 330 miles (530 km) in diameter.

Space drones help scientists study Earth's atmosphere and outer space. Scientists are also working on drones to explore other planets and asteroids. Asteroids are large rocks that orbit the sun. Some space drones are large like the X-37B. Others are much smaller. Scientists want to send multiple drones to space at once.

Primary Source

Scientist Håvard Grip works for the National Aeronautics and Space Administration (NASA). He explained how NASA could use drones:

> *In the future, we could imagine doing things like . . . exploration using multiple [drones] or going to inaccessible areas.*

Source: Mike Wall. "Propelling Exploration: Drones Are Going Interplanetary." *Space.com*, 28 June 2019, space.com. Accessed 22 Oct. 2019.

Comparing Texts

Think about the quote. Does it support the information in this chapter? Or does it give a different perspective? Explain how in a few sentences.

Engineers tested the Mars 2020 rover at NASA's Jet Propulsion Laboratory in December 2019.

CHAPTER 2

Why Use Drones?

Drones have changed the way scientists explore space. The National Aeronautics and Space Administration (NASA) uses space drones. NASA also uses rovers. It has sent rovers to explore the surface of Mars. Rovers are robots with wheels.

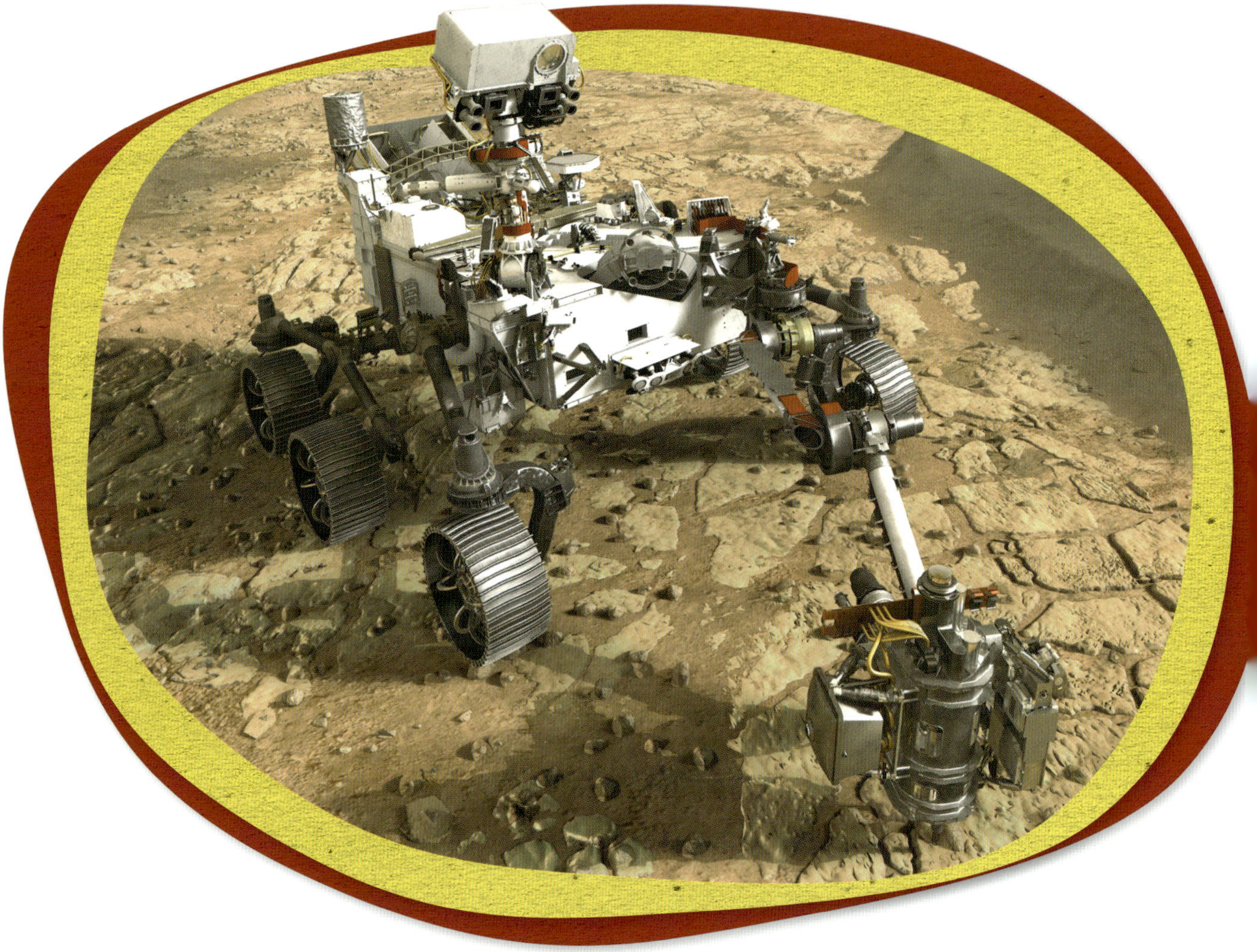

This graphic shows the Mars 2020 rover, which will drill into Mars and collect samples.

Like drones, rovers are mostly autonomous. This means they can do things by themselves. For example, they can self-navigate. Rovers and drones have **sensors**. Sensors can find objects in their path. Then the rover or drone can avoid those objects.

Rovers versus Drones

Drones can go places rovers cannot go. Rovers cannot reach some areas. For example, drones can explore steep hillsides and **craters**. Rovers fall over if the ground is too steep. They cannot get back up.

Who's Flying This Thing?

People use remote controls to operate some drones. These devices send messages to drones through **radio waves**. But remote controls do not work with many space drones. Radio waves take several minutes to travel from Earth to other planets. So most space drones need to be autonomous.

Rovers run on solar power. This means they get energy from sunlight. This makes it difficult for rovers to explore areas where there is no sunlight. Drones can explore these areas. This is because they do not only run on solar power. Drones have batteries. They recharge their batteries at a landing craft. The landing craft is the spacecraft that brings the drones to the planet.

Rovers have no way to get back to Earth after their mission is done. They remain in space. But drones can return to Earth on a landing craft.

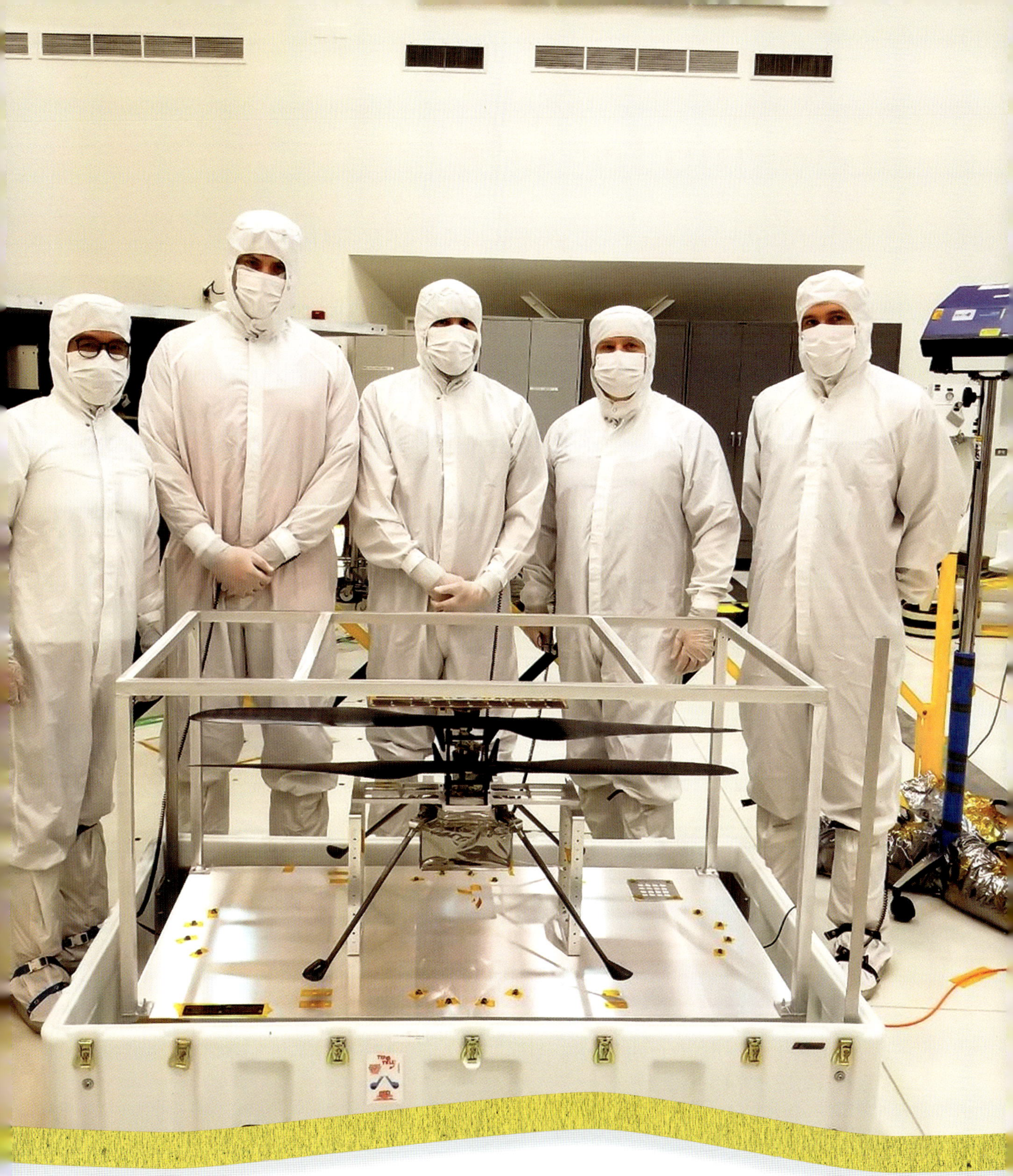

Many NASA engineers and technicians work together to build drones.

Looking for Life

Scientists have not yet found life on other planets. They are looking for locations that can support life. Life can be tiny. It does not have to be other human-like creatures. Scientists can use drones to search for signs of life on other planets and moons.

NASA researchers test some vehicles on Devon Island in Canada because its environment is similar to the surface of Mars.

Titan's atmosphere is thick. This will make it easy for a drone to fly around Titan.

NASA is building a new drone called the *Dragonfly*. This drone's mission will be to explore Titan. Titan is one of Saturn's moons. NASA plans to launch the *Dragonfly* in 2026.

This graphic shows how the *Dragonfly* drone will land on Titan.

Scientists sent a spacecraft to study Titan. The spacecraft took pictures of Titan. Scientists studied these images. They discovered that Titan has clouds and rain. It also has lakes, rivers, and an ocean. These are signs that there may be life on Titan.

Drone Technology

Titan is the second-largest known moon in our solar system. There is a lot of land to explore. Rovers are not ideal. For example, rovers on Mars have only explored a small part of the planet's surface. The *Dragonfly* could fly much greater distances than a rover can travel.

Diagram of a Space Drone

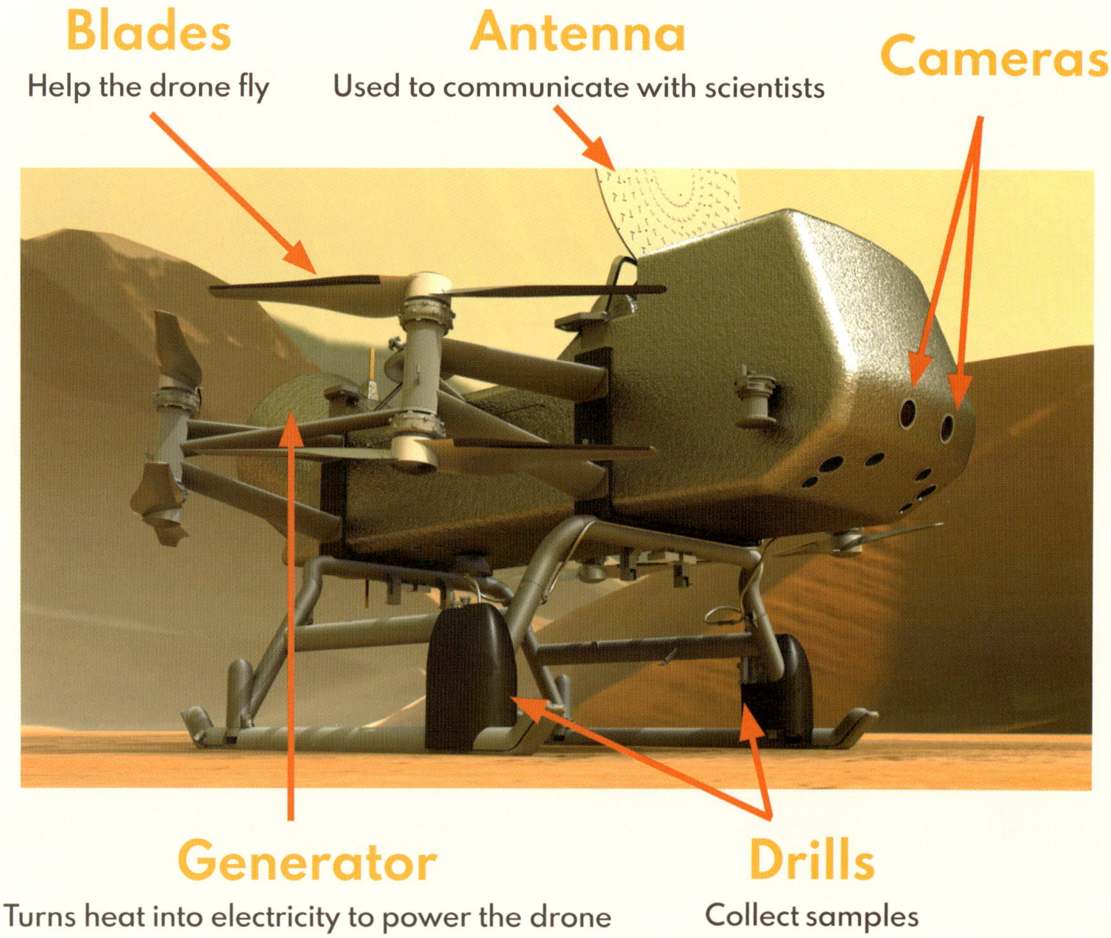

This diagram shows the parts of a *Dragonfly* drone. The drone has blades like a helicopter. It also has parts that help it collect data.

NASA hopes the *Dragonfly* will explore Titan for more than ten years. The drone would land on the surface of this moon. Titan is full of **radioactive** material. This type of material produces heat. The *Dragonfly* will have special technology. The technology will turn the heat into electricity. The electricity will recharge the drone's batteries.

Further Evidence

Look at the website below. What evidence from the site supports what you learned in Chapter Two?

Titan

abdocorelibrary.com/space-drones

NASA is building and testing different versions of the Extreme Access Flyer drone.

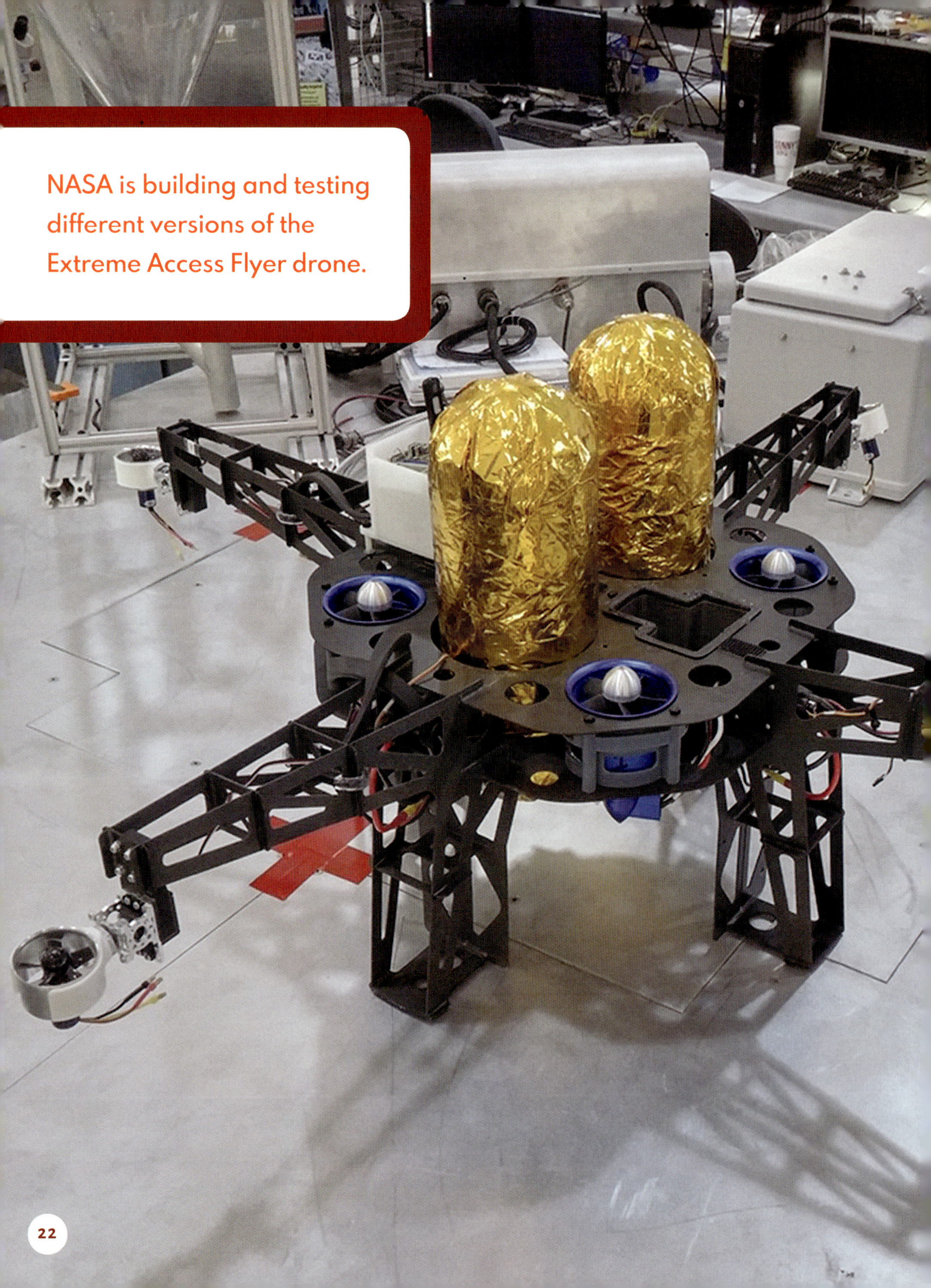

CHAPTER 3

The Future of Space Drones

Future space drones will have improved technology. They will be able to work in more extreme places. For example, NASA is making a drone called an Extreme Access Flyer (EAF). EAFs could explore craters on planets and asteroids.

EAFs would use jets of oxygen or water vapor as fuel. The jets could spray in different directions to steer the drones. EAFs could use the water vapor or other gases available on a planet. That way, they would not run out of fuel.

EAFs could fly in and out of craters. Scientists believe there are important resources in craters,

Finding Shelter

Scientists hope future space drones will be able to explore lava tubes. Lava tubes are large underground tunnels formed from volcanoes. The tubes could give astronauts shelter. Mars has an extreme **environment**. It is far from the sun. It gets very cold. The lava tubes could provide protection.

NASA is working on a flying robot called Shapeshifter. It will be able to change shape to explore different environments on Titan.

including water. EAFs could collect rock samples from craters. Scientists will study these samples to learn more about craters.

The *Mars Helicopter Scout* will have a camera that can take high-quality images.

The *Mars Helicopter Scout*

Scientists hope rovers and drones will be able to work together in the future. NASA is building a drone called the JPL *Mars Helicopter Scout*. This drone could be used alongside a rover to study Mars. The rover will collect samples.

The *Mars Helicopter Scout* will have cameras and sensors. The drone could alert the rover if there were obstacles in the rover's path.

Space drones perform important tasks. They can help collect samples. Scientists use samples to find out what objects in space are made of. With the help of drones, it is possible that astronauts will be able to explore and perhaps even live on other planets someday.

Explore Online

Visit the website below. Did you learn any new information about space exploration that wasn't in Chapter Three?

Why Do We Care about Water on Mars?

abdocorelibrary.com/space-drones

Drone Stats

X-37B

- Orbits Earth
- Used by the US Air Force
- Could be used to bring experiments back from space

Extreme Access Flyer

- Could explore craters on asteroids and planets
- Could collect rock samples

JPL *Mars Helicopter Scout*

- Could work with rovers
- Could scan paths for obstacles

Glossary

atmosphere
the layer of gases that separates the surface of a planet from space

craters
holes formed when something hits a planet or an asteroid

environment
the things and surroundings that are all around one, such as water or air

orbit
to travel in a circle around a planet, star, or other large object in space

radio waves
waves that are used to send information over distances to radios, televisions, and other devices

radioactive
giving off a powerful type of energy

sensors
equipment that can detect things such as heat, light, sound, and pressure

Online Resources

To learn more about space drones, visit our free resource websites below.

Core Library CONNECTION
FREE! COMMON CORE MULTIMEDIA RESOURCES

Visit **abdocorelibrary.com** or scan this QR code for free Common Core resources for teachers and students, including vetted activities, multimedia, and booklinks, for deeper subject comprehension.

Booklinks NONFICTION NETWORK
FREE! ONLINE NONFICTION RESOURCES

Visit **abdobooklinks.com** or scan this QR code for free additional online weblinks for further learning. These links are routinely monitored and updated to provide the most current information available.

Learn More

Doudna, Kelly. *Space Exploration*. Abdo Publishing, 2017.

Mars: Explore the Mysteries of the Red Planet. DK, 2020.

McCarthy, Cecilia Pinto. *Military Drones*. Abdo Publishing, 2021.

Index

About the Author

Martha London writes books for young readers full-time. When she isn't writing, you can find her hiking in the woods.